Lauren Davis's hardwe[...]
brim over with rumination, rhythm, and reaction.[...]
as church light," these poems showcase frustrations and deep-rooted hungers so authentically human we almost catch the heartbeat's throb in each line we ghost over. "I wait at the forest's edge," says Davis, "eager, out in the clearing," and we can't help but want to join her.

ELIJAH BURRELL
author of *Troubler* and *The Skin of the River*

In *Home Beneath the Church*, Lauren Davis brings us into the landscape of body through images from the natural world. Poem after gorgeous poem, she carefully shows how one's past can cause harm, but there are cures in the world around us—"I have crossed one ocean to heal/at the hem of your skirts." Davis has become one of my favorite poets for her fresh images, her engaging voice, and her absolutely exceptional ability to do so much in a small space. *Home Beneath the Church* is a collection of beauty and grace. These well-crafted poems are perfect gems in their brilliance and in their questioning of our temporary lives and environments around us: "How many graves have we danced on? How many secrets does each stone keep?" Lauren Davis is the poet you need to be reading; I am forever in awe of her work, and this stunning collection left me so thankful she is writing poems.

KELLI RUSSELL AGODON
author of *Dialogues with Rising Tides*

Ever since I first encountered Lauren Davis's exquisite poetry, I have longed for her first full-length collection. With its incantations about how a woman resides within the (un)holy rooms of her body's longings and belongings, *Home Beneath the Church* crafts a home, a sanctuary, for any reader to cohabitate with the language of the prismatic familial and sacred. I am grateful now to be able to visit Davis's debut abode.

SANDRA YANNONE
author of *Boats for Women*

"There once was a wolf in me," Lauren Davis warns us in *Home Beneath the Church*, preparing us for poems that, like wolves, trust their own instincts. These are poems that darken in the light the way rainworks painted on the sidewalk are activated by rain. They stand up humbly before a deeply intimate backdrop to exorcise demons of family and body. These are poems of reverence and fury to both monuments and small gestures of the body. These are poems of faith in the face of faithlessness. Every part of nature—the lover, the moon, snow, the sky, hummingbirds mating, a herd of elks—is worshipped on these pages. Davis is a poet who cannot name her sins without offering them her tears.

RISA DENENBERG
author of *slight faith*

Home Beneath the Church

Lauren Davis

Fernwood
PRESS

Home Beneath the Church

©2022 by Lauren Davis

Fernwood Press
Newberg, Oregon
www.fernwoodpress.com

Cover and page design: Mareesa Fawver Moss

Cover image: Will Swann on Unsplash

Printed in the United States of America

ISBN 978-1-59498-081-7

for Charlie

Contents

I.

The Estranged

It is not by chance when my body returns
to me. I called her through each season,
teasing out her name in late light.

I was never one for foreign languages.
I tangled the *r*'s and *l*'s of her until I learned
to relax my silences around her tongue.

The new moon sinks into the monkshood's fur,
and I think of the day I first found
my body incapable of prayer. I did not ask her

for what she could not do,
and now she shelters me
with a wolfsbane clutch unfolding.

Come touch
us with bare hands.
I dare you.

To Make Smaller

The jeweler left a depression
where my engagement ring had been cut
to size. For weeks I worried the thing
like a rosary in famine. I did not know
what to do. Take it back, let it go,
find another smith? Morning,
while driving, I knew. I wanted you,
mother—my third gone lung—
to handle the matter. Heading south, I hit
a sparrow. In my rearview mirror,
it tossed on pavement, willing itself
to fly again. *Out of nowhere.*
Isn't that what people always say?

Watch Over the Woodstove by Day

At night, the dark and I
take our turn. A few
damp sticks. One more log.

Out there, an owl stalks
silent. Snow hunts air.
Darling, I did not mean

to bring you such cold. Sleep.
And I will fill this cabin
with the black beast's heat.

Home

Frightening the foliage from its sleep, we travel along
the Quinault Lake Loop in our big red truck.

Roofed by dank rainforest, we know
we are not alone, though we see no bird, no beast.

You say, *It's beautiful, but do we really belong here
where creatures hide?* Then an elk herd stomps across

the dirt road, and you brake, shocked. The fattest turns
to stare over his long beard. To know or warn us.

Yes, my love, we belong, but on soil-stained knees,
asking for each wild thing's consent to stand.

Vulvodynia

What church boasts a door unyielding
to the devout? More than a barrier
to the cold, it must unbolt. I remember

when they pinpointed my body's faulty
piece—my vulva's vestibule. *Same name
for the opening to a church*, you said.

But you're refused your seat of worship,
singing hymns in the snow. Inside, the incense
and sanctity go stale. Can a building grieve?

I am grieving, needing to bless and be blessed,
the church refusing the will of its Lord.

My Body Incapable

Anything to let you in, I sat for all the doctors.
I trembled on their examination tables, tore the white paper.

Graduate students thrusted fingers inside,
noted the spasms, their eyes not on mine.

Vulvodynia, vulvar vestibulitis, vaginismus—
they sound like names of fragile flowers.

The lamps turned up, you hover over the kitchen sink,
searching for shards of glass. You feel through

plates and dinner scraps, the shattered tumbler trashed
and bagged. When you deem the kitchen safe, you join me

in the bedroom. You've secured our shelter—
candles snuffed, doors locked. But what of you?

I cannot make love tonight. It hurts too much.
I beg you to me. My thighs clasp you out.

Forever, you say, *we have forever to wait.*

In the Forest by the Bay

"...the McMillin family still holds vigil, in a mysterious monument
hidden in the woods. Each seat contains the ashes of a family member,
and the structure holds many symbols as well."
—Anne Erickson

Alone, we enter the gate and round the stairs to stand
beside a limestone table made for seven chairs.

Gray beard, furrows, arthritic feet.
I know enough to know I must imagine

you dead. Every day has its own
grief, understanding we cannot go on this way—

living. As a child you would play
here with your brother, unaware

that each chair houses human ash.
Is this why you revere all things, just in case—

cup of tea, nick in my stocking, fireplace?
How many graves have we danced on?

How many secrets does each stone keep? Look
what we have done to even the mummies, splitting

open their sleep, spoiling their chances. Each time
a new line appears on your face, I thank God

for making me witness. We circle the table
cleared of its dishes. The two of us beached

on the gravesite, you slip your mouth over mine.
I have no brick to lay, no land on which to build

you a tomb. Undomed, open to the gathering rain.
I love you most when you comment on the sky.

Hemlock Has Taken a Lover

How does she smell in winter, summer?
The moon winks behind her many limbs.

Did you court her—mating call strung
in wind's teeth? Bodies pollinating

in this and each long hour?

Cathedral

Lichen scented—deadfalls' punk awakens
in rain. I am not sure how else to be but yours.

Crows name us beneath branches.
My body rises, feral. Cloudburst dirties

your cheeks. Undersong
of wayward fronds.

And in the forest, you are scripture and priest.
And in the forest, wild roses tuck their leaves.

Botany

Drought runs as a headline. Crops mature off season,
keeping farmers courting their fields with desperate

attention, dissolution threatened in limp stalks.
I thought, beyond the glass, my tree was a tree

with no discernible attributes, a toss-away seed
that found a home and stretched, providing a thread of privacy.

This year lacks wonderment. Holes have been dug,
and I am too tired to fill them. But on that tree—nondescript

thing of wilted leaves that has never revealed its name—
hangs a single slash of red, a kiss of a cherry,

asking to be left or harvested,
I must decide—I have only one.

Cabin in the Pines

I have resigned myself to pain.
Bathing outside with you, what is that

behind the trees—a neighbor's lamp?
We wait to see if it might climb.

Stars peek from beneath trembling trees,
flirt with our stripped bodies. If pain's reprieve

approached tonight, what would I do?
I could stay with you and open here

in the blushing light, let you wonder
about the curious new way I toss my hair.

Moon, her insatiable appetite for altitude—
she rises, shows her turned face.

Mountain, Incidental

I would if I could bed you now, but the birch trees.
If you had seen how they stand, side by side

like rooted revenants, you'd know.
They nearly informed of other worlds.

I am without fault, my car in the ditch. The ice
appeared beyond a bend. The elevation felt minor.

Have faith, I am only temporarily mislaid.
I tread down the mountainside in the rain.

Vaginismus

Sugar on the tongue,
we have many hours to waste
without complete touch.

Nothing can touch the way
you could if I could
take you without pain.

What is this body if I cannot—
when full of desire—join with a man?
I have waited so long to find you.

I told the sky prayers. And the sky
listened. When I fell out of the trees,
strangers showed me

where you dwelled. Now that I
have brought myself to you
I cannot bring myself to you fully.

Sugar on our lips. It does not matter.
Beloved, one day I will open. You will hear
the rush of my footsteps approaching,

though you lie beside me.

To My Pelvic Floor Physical Therapist

I pursued you for so long. Bend between my knees
and ask, *May I*, before noting the grade of my pain.
And here? Does it hurt here?

Court from my muscles a new song with your little jellied digits.
No one has contemplated more than you my body's grief.
No one else has mapped my shadowed lands.

Work like a cat coaxing her kitten from a well. Call me out
of the tremoring murk, my body received. Curious woman,
sit beside me here at my hospital cot and draw back these pale sheets.

While Boys Get First Kisses

A displaced coyote pup lingers
in our gravel drive. They took
her trees to pay for a new school.

Early frost this year—it spreads
its mouth over each downed leaf
in our small patch of earth.

> *Little pup, I cannot build you a shelter.*
> *My fingers are uneducated things. And in my bed*
> *you could sleep if not for your teeth.*

Down the road children turn cartwheels.
A little boy receives his first kiss. Blushing,
he cries, and the whole schoolyard turns.

They hear a hammering. They see poles
raised and naked, awaiting black scaffolding.
Construction men move as crows.

> *Little kit, follow your mother to some unmarked*
> *den. In the brush, I see her flare of rust.*
> *Forgive me, my useless hands.*

Land Not Required

Make a sailor out of me.
I have been landlocked for so long
on my little black beach,
braiding kelp, christening seagulls.

Your sloop stretches out of the gloom,
sighting my shore. Anchored, salt
in the crease of your wrists. My body
unaccustomed to the sway of water,

first rock me back and forth on sand.
Train me how to hike the mast.
In the berth, let me map oceans
on your chest. I will follow you

anywhere. We will test the theory
of the flat earth, in the morning waking
to a hull of muddled latitudes,
the helm each night unattended.

I Will Cocoon You

Allow me for a season your reeded form.
Let me create for you another name,

a new body—if you'll trust my body
fastened to the world with a slick of your silk.

When I am finished, friends will call you
stranger. My common crow butterfly,

come, and I will leave you with wings
stiff with blood, leathery. Roam

petal to petal, seeking again the silver
warmth of my chrysalis skins.

In the Arms of the Rhône Delta

When I unbraid my hair, listen for moonlight
on the eyelids of white horses. If they wanted us
enough, they could clear the strung fence,
the shallow creek where daystars dream.

Our small bed in the small white hut
with the white cross at its crest—here sings
soft rain, the sound of one dove's sleep broken
by darker berries bursting open.

I am a New Caledonian Owlet-Nightjar

Unseen since 1998,
I am nearly a lost breed.

No one has heard my voice but you—
a different genus of bird
who sought and discovered me.

I beat my wings against yours
unable to mate, but look

how groomed my semiplumes.
I pluck them into dead air.

Now I am ready
to be collected beneath
your breast.

Let scientists say I dared to survive—
that you came down from your perch

to quiver against me,
my last known touch.

They will find me in the brushwood,
virgin. But a song in my throat.

II.

Mother Says

I am not your mother, dark and strange.
My orphan, I am sorry. In some countries
the seasons refuse to change.

If I could, I would force the clouds to misarrange,
but they stack like dead men in anthologies.
I am not your mother, dark and strange.

I have heard of a thing called spring where rage
only shows its face in the blood of berries.
The seasons refuse to change.

I am small hands, a deranged
child picking through ghost bodies.
I am not your mother, dark and strange.

Gods delay, slow to make days age.
I strike beads of rosaries.
The seasons refuse to change.

I cannot show you the weather's range
when my sky echoes your sky. My apologies,
I am not your mother, dark and strange.
The seasons refuse to change.

My Hierophant

Lecture me, love, on the feminine archetype
tattooed on the center of your breastbone.

Tell me of your father who, at your birth,
purchased a gold medallion—the Madonna

and child—and how you decided
she must be a permanent stain on your skin.

Allow me to hold space here at your chest,
to listen differently. My education is incomplete.

How old is that ink? The lines have started
to bleed. Did you choose to pen her in coal

for simplicity, or did you want her different—
a Black Madonna? She is ancient, the Kali-Mother.

Traditions bend their knees to her—the Buddhists,
Hindus, Haitian Voodooists, Christians hiding her

with theories of her darkness: *It is the result of incense,*
the chemistry of stone. She is because she is.

In the sanctity of your sheets, guide me
back. List her names for me.

Sun Wound

I watch hummingbirds mating
off season, their touch delicate
as church light.

Nearby, their nest anchored
with spider spit on the pine's thinnest
branch. I want one day to have the faith

of the smallest thing,
to build a home on slight
land. In the worst of the year's heat,

I string prayer along my skin
and request any other fever.
If the hummingbirds sing

halleluiah, how can I ever hear
over the sound of my own heart
protesting the sun, the sun?

Touring the French Basilica

Around us throngs of children twist to learn each stone and saint,
their limbs jerking with the labor of reverence. Somewhere, chanting.

Stained glass claws its way to beams, pope-blessed. You lower
your camera, cap the lens. You say, *I just have to put it in my brain.*

The longer we stand, the more prayerful each visitor mutates.
We might as well be stone ourselves.

Except the woman barely beyond the north facade—
she stomps her foot to scatter pigeons, pops her gum.

Inside, silent as candle flame. Outside,

a clash of wings.

I Have Forgotten an Important Thing

The demon told me his name
in the dream. To know his name
is to control him, my beloved said.

I cannot remember it, just as I cannot
remember most things—each home
I have lived in, why the dark still scares me.

I could do so much with a demon.
I'd have a bit of company on nights
I won't sleep. He'd tell me stories,

and I would be such a polite listener.
I wonder if he'd get cold here,
if he'd tire of taking the stairs.

I'm sure he'd dislike my cat.
Still, I would like to have a demon.
I will go back to bed now, try again.

Pilgrimage to Saint Sara

Down in the crypt, you lift her skirts.
I wait for you above, wandering
tight streets, spending our few coins.

I must give you appropriate time.
I do not rush you, as you did not rush me
when I entered her home beneath the church.

Feel it when you arrive—the heat
from the candles hits at the last step.
Her grotto holds another hemisphere

where even smoke makes shadows. At my visit,
I watched Romanies fingering the flamingo pink
and gold gowns drowning her small frame.

Three jeweled crowns on her head. She swelled
with silk. Grown men wept. Little girls kissed
her toes. I looked into her eyes and felt nothing.

In hushed tones I tried to call her forth. And then,
when for a moment Sara and I stood alone,
I placed two fingers from my lips then hers.

Do the same. See why I came to you
last night disrobing not only my clothes.
Touch her. Know her. Then to me, new, return.

To Saint Sara During Her Procession

Canticles and skin
crowd the cultus at the beach.
They must bathe your feet.
Strong men on four white horses
lower you into the sea.

With painted-open
eyes, you look after your kind
congregated at
your silk-encrusted frame.
With peregrine tongue, I pray.

Have I not been good?
I crossed one ocean to heal
at the hem of your skirts.
Dark Mother, sprung from the shore,
may one more orphan be yours?

Put Me to Sleep

Chef slams the skillet down, yells for eggs.
Four tickets in my apron means he'll need
another carton. Not that I'll fetch it for him.
I stay on my side of the kitchen.

One time, a nurse said Saddam Hussein saved
bread crusts for the birds. In jail, without
the distracting temptation of dictatorship,
he watered dusty plants, another's task.

I dated an ex-con. On the anniversary
of his mother's death, I saw him walking
out of town to her grave. She was buried one
state over. Months later, he raped me.

The Dalai Lama said, *Aggression is an intimate*
part of ourselves. Also, *It's well known*
that good feelings only cause boredom
and gently put you to sleep.

Like people don't know the price of fruit, Chef says,
when I hand him a ticket for a yogurt parfait.
I scoop raspberries out of the plastic tub.
Jesus Christ, he says and slaps my hand away.

You have to take the ones from the top first,
or the others below bruise beneath their weight.
His calloused fingers cradle each berry—
not unlike a father tender with his newborn.

Honestly

There once was a wolf in me.
If I had been born a man,
I might have done all the things
done to me.

I thought sex was power—
men kept taking it because they had more of it.

But I came as a girl.
A blame between my thighs. Tell me, daughters,

I am good. Tell me again.

Camargue Horse Knows

You feed the fenced white horse
hay found at your feet. His teeth
so large, I protest he'll bite my hand.

Don't curl your fist, you say.
Open palmed. I find a lengthy weed,
hold it out far as if it might catch flame.

He stomps, tosses his head, backs away.
You scared him, you tell me. *He thinks
it's a whip.* I try to coax the horse back, explain.

Remember when you first offered me
your long, willing body—the gift
an instinct. I shook at the threat of it.

The horse returns to you,
hungry, head bowed.

The Moon Is Dead

Which is why tides rise and do not halt
at sleeping horses. Which is why water
confuses itself for land and makes

valleys of itself for beasts to graze.
There is no time for elegy or investigation
into the origins of this death. Though I assume

loneliness or, scientifically speaking,
a fatal longing for the moon's rock to be warmed
by the bellies of horses dreaming.

The Anchoress

Entombed, they buried me
ritually. Brick by brick I became

Christ's eternal bride
in the pelvis of the church.

Three windows. One to receive
bread. Another for the world.

A small slit to take communion.
I own a crucifix. I own an altar.

I own my grave.
Here, I am more permanent

than the sun. I never leave
over that last hill.

Each day, my bare hands hold
the dirt of my death bed.

If they had built me a door,
I would have opened the door.

Tell Me

Who do I talk to about my loneliness?
Even the grass has hidden beneath the snow.

Cloud-leaden, I cannot find the sky's right eye.
There's enough time in this day for grief,

but I return each hour to its fold.
Tomorrow, a downpour.

Cave Study

What exhausted spider slogs along inside
my body, assembling her last home?

If you seek me, love, you will catch
at my cave's mouth, rip her long assignment.

Overwhelm the web—I am full of faith.
Search my grotto's fingertips, silked.

Traverse out of sunlight's last slit.

Whiteout

I have done worse things than startle
the waxwing from seed I flung atop the snow.
I cannot name these without weeping.

In deep winter I am alone with myself.
Branches startle the roof. They sound
like footsteps. I think it has finally

come for me. Clouds empty their bones.

III.

Pearled

Mother, my first love,
I hang your betrayal
around my throat pearl strung.

I have heard more of me exists
than the estate of my neck,
but who could care

with the pearls swelling here
asking to be sucked,

sunk into the black, black sea,
back to the mouths of mollusks
who wait for what you

have thieved from their hushed tongues,
from their deep rest
where the mud's secrets breathe.

Mother, Dark and Near

Everywhere—stranger, chorus girl,
burl in the hickory. I paint my eyes

in the morning black, and out
of the magician's hat, I am you.

Smithed at your coals—your fingerprints
a maker's mark all over my lips.

You are the God and the garden
and the apple tree. You dragged me up

from the wanting seed. I am nothing
if not your daughter. I am nothing

without your haunt—heavy, annulling
the holy Father. Possessed, in you

I am kept. Mother, in you
all my days wax, wane night-blessed.

Stark Hollow Farm

What bird weaves a nest inches
from the dirt? Trusts their young
to an earth with creatures like myself,

fumbling about, photographing mountains
that shadow lesser mountains?
Where is everyone? Only moss

on this rock. Myself on the other.
And when did I last lie in a field so empty
the wind startled me, bringing the scent

of beasts in heat? Who cares so little
that they litter the woods? I reach for the paper.
My hands fill with bleached blossoms.

I Didn't Know Snow Then

Flakes fell all over me
as I flitted to the meeting.

I felt a new type of beautiful.
Baptized in iced wax.

Men turned to look.
Women shook their heads.

Albino peacock, I sauntered
into the office, and chairs swiveled.

In the glass pane, I checked
my cheeks, five wild rivers

of mascara severing my smile.
Remarkable how I can walk

cut up through my hours,
and no one speaks of it.

Every Sunday at the Grocery Store

Your ex-wife buys a bouquet,
unaware of my stare as I stock
shelves. You may have failed

to tell her of me. I've never
grasped what to do when flowers
start wilting—to press them,

compost them, throw them
in the sea. She knows,
her skirt an extravagant

bloom in the gust of a closing door.

On the Deck

Your neck bent to let me shave the soft hairs
above your collar line. The gesture
of the blade like one lick of a wave reshaping

the beach a few steps from our door. How the water
at the bay's edge takes a handful of stones each time it retreats.
Boats motor by, kicking up a surge, more sand stretched

and remade, man's handprints on each silt's grain.
A crow finds his dish in the husk of a washed-up crab.
A silver fish shows his face. I landscape you

fine as the sandcastles of lords. I open the topography
of your neck to the sun's burn, my kiss.
Raise your chin, king, and reclaim your country.

At Dusk I Walk Home Through the Field

After closing, my coworker lifted lavender
from the bouquet resting
atop the compost.
For my dog's grave, she said.

Lavandula, use for: sleep,
sadness, mummification. Mother
Mary anointing her son's feet,
drying them with her hair.

Let me wrap your hands in the scent
of those shivering stalks, preserve
your body beneath stars and distant howls.
Meet me in the yard.

Gambling on Sunday

We nick the wood of our new
kitchen table with casino dice.

I am ahead by a few
and done with the roast.

I thought the lake effect
would keep us from snow,

but ice takes the bay,
weds our windowpanes.

Today I uncover
the last of my luck.

From here on out, it's just
hard work and collard greens.

But long days of your hands
and longer days of white.

It Is Good to Eat Oranges in Winter

Return, and my hands
will be a loud orchard.

Snow gathering
at the window. But citrus

in our mouths. It is enough
to have two glad seasons

entangled in sheets, enough
to believe in.

It Happened Beside Us

I read of the crime
while crumpling old newspapers
for your anniversary gift.
A man traveled here to murder,
following the demand of angels.

Beside our home, down
the deer's trodden path,
with one hand he dragged
a man, in the other
a knife.

It happened on a Sunday.
Months have passed.
No trial yet, not another word,
and surely the blood
washed deep into the mud.

I have slept so well since that day.
I have cooked many meals,
kissed you many times.
Felt no heartache.
Unaware, unaware.

Growing up, my mother joked
a butterfly would distract
me from wildfire. I would never
see flames, just soft wing beats.
It is better this way.

If I Were a Resurrection Fern

And you the wind-whipped rain,
I'd draw you up. My fronds bright soaked

without shame. Imagine my grief this past
drought. I shivered in my little

plot of lack. Come my mineral nip,
my sky-dropped lake.

Nothing can keep us apart,
not even climate nor gods.

You come down and down
and never stop coming down,

and I revive, baptized.

Walking the Lakota People's Land

At the abandoned sweat lodge, prayer ties
float in the sapling frames.

Colorful as fish, they snap at the wind.
Sundancers came and went last month.

The air feels thick with otherness. I trespass, aware.
I find a fallen cloth square on the footpath

and desire it as a souvenir, fingering its coarse
thread, then placing it back among the stones.

I do not belong where blackberries grow
in deep clumps. I grab at them, losing many

in the overgrowth. I stuff my face, glance over
my shoulder where one fence unbolts.

But Most of All

Beloved, never not ever will I braid
your absence through my hair.
I will not accept the single-bodied bed.

I hear you in the ceiling. Your breath
fogs the dark. Why did I come here
where your body could not go?

Remember when I brought you to the woods
to show you my owls? How quickly they
greeted you, coiling down from the trees

before we even turned the trail. How small
my heart that I felt jealousy then.
Each day I leave the cabin and wait

for the orcas, off season. Madronas
undress their layers, so that I might gaze
a little longer. I keep a piece

of fossilized wood that matches yours.
I hold it to my lips. But most of all I am
a woman in communion, her ear to the wall.

To Craft the Bracken Boat

For you I construct
a boat out of leaves.
In my harbors it waits tucked.

Each bine and grass plucked
before the winter thieves.
For you I construct.

Sheets of water shucked.
The day's light recedes.
In my harbors it waits tucked.

Its bract body bucked
as your breath around it weaves.
For you I construct.

The last of sun sucked
below these wound sheaves.
In my harbors it waits tucked.

Invite this waiting helm to be rucked
in the dark of all your eves.
For you I construct.
In my harbors it waits tucked.

Creatured

I lay where deer lay
each night, where grass
bends like light. Warmth
gummed to the earth.

For each lustful tick, my skin
explicit. I am a feast, famine's finish.
My blood honest, body ready
on the glade's bruised mud.

Beloved, were we ever this wild?
Were we ever two beasts
mated beneath the prying sun?
Let us remember those rude bodies.

I will be fur for you. I am hoof
for you. I am on all fours for you.
I wait at the forest's edge,
eager, out in the clearing.

Acknowledgments

I have much gratitude for the publications in which variations of these poems first appeared:

Angel City Review: "Touring the French Basilica"

Borderlands: Texas Poetry Review: "Sun Wound"

Calliope: "Land Not Required"

Crab Orchard Review: "Pilgrimage to Saint Sara"

Ibbetson Street: "Walking the Lakota People's Land"

Mojave Heart Review: "Watch Over the Woodstove," "At Dusk I Walk Home through the Field"

New Contrast: "I am a New Caledonian Owlet-Nightjar"

Ninth Letter: "In the Forest by the Bay"

Obra: "Vulvodynia"

Panoplyzine: "Mother, Dark and Near," "I Didn't Know Snow Then"

Pidgeonholes: "Cathedral," "Creatured"

Pilgrimage Magazine: "Whiteout"

Poet Lore: "The Estranged"

Qu: "Put Me to Sleep"

Rabid Oak: "Hemlock Has Taken a Lover"

Semaphore Magazine: "Stark Hollow Farm," "Mother Says"

A Shadow Map: An Anthology by Survivors of Sexual Assault: "Camargue Horse Knows"

Sinking City Lit Mag: "Botany"

Stoneboat Literary Journal: "My Hierophant"

Sun Star Lit: "My Body Incapable," "To Saint Sara During Her Procession"

Tar River Poetry: "Every Sunday at the Grocery Store"

"Every Sunday at the Grocery Store" was reprinted in *The Inspired Poet* (Two Sylvias Press). "Land Not Required" was reprinted in the anthology *You Can Hear the Ocean* (Brighton Press).

"The moon is dead" is a quote from Carl Jung's *The Red Book*.

Many of these poems first appeared in the chapbook *Each Wild Thing's Consent* (Poetry Wolf Press).

I am endlessly blessed to have such generous teachers and friends in my life. Without you, these poems would have never been written.

Eric Muhr, who believed in this work and gave it a home. Mareesa Fawver Moss, who shaped this book into its material being. Jan Bailey and George Singleton, who first helped me find my voice. Mark Wunderlich, Timothy Liu, David Daniel, April Bernard, and Major Jackson, who showed me what it is to be a poet in the world. The Writers' Workshoppe, which gave me a writing family on another coast. Risa Denenberg, Jayne Marek, Kelli Russell Agodon, and Ronda Broatch—the forever big-hearted Upstairs Poets. Hypatia-in-the-Woods, and the silence it delivered. Lauren Brazeal and Barrett Warner, whose close readings breathed life into earlier drafts of this book. Hannah Ohlson and Michelle Oppenheimer, for your meticulous proofing. Jeremey Flick and Poetry Wolf Press, who lovingly championed many of these poems. My sister poet Meaghan Quinn, a woman that inspires me to stay true. I am honored to walk this path with you. Anna and Peter Quinn. Samantha Ladwig and Thom. The writers Elijah Burrell, Sandra Yannone, Jennifer Porter, Maura Snell, Pam Dionne, Judy Borenin, Joanne Clarkson, Laura Schaeffer, Bill Carty, Denton Loving, and Elaine Fletcher Chapman—your words are a gift to us all. Kathryn Hunt, kind friend, thank you. Tamah Augen and Rene Schwiesow, such loving souls. Father and Karla, mother, Justin, Caleb. And those unnamed.

And my forever beloved, Charlie. You are every poem. Every flower. Each kind moment. Before you, the moon was just a moon.

God, Goddess, the One that Listens. I asked and You answered.

Title Index

First Line Index